Ekke

Ekke

KLARA DU PLESSIS

Copyright © 2018 Klara du Plessis

All rights reserved

Palimpsest Press
1171 Eastlawn Ave.
Windsor, Ontario. N8S 3J1
www.palimpsestpress.ca

Book and cover design by Kate Hargreaves (CorusKate Design)
Cover image: "Vela Sikubhekile" by Nandipha Mntambo
Cover photograph courtesy of the Stevenson Gallery, South Africa
Edited by Jim Johnstone

Palimpsest Press would like to thank the Canada Council for the Arts, and the Ontario Arts Council for their support of our publishing program. We also acknowledge the assistance of the Government of Ontario through the Ontario Book Publishing Tax Credit.

 Canada Council for the Arts Conseil des Arts du Canada  ONTARIO ARTS COUNCIL CONSEIL DES ARTS DE L'ONTARIO Ontario

Library and Archives Canada Cataloguing in Publication

Du Plessis, Klara, 1988-, author
Ekke / Klara du Plessis.

Poems.
Includes some text in Afrikaans.
ISBN 978-1-926794-71-6 (softcover)

I. Title.

PS8607.U17E45 2018   C811'.6   C2017-907127-0

PRINTED AND BOUND IN CANADA

Vir Dorothea Vermeulen

CONTENTS

First of all we no longer write in black	9
Stillframe Inbox	17
Las Meninas	25
Ekke	31
Conveyor Belt	41
Hunter-Gatherer Criminals	53
Ceiling Roses	63
Someone other than else	71
Translations	81
Notes	86
Acknowledgements	87

1

FIRST OF ALL WE NO LONGER WRITE IN BLACK BUT IN WHITE STONES.

In small towns on South African outskirts,
names are outlined in whitewashed stones, packed
on hillsides to spell,
to welcome,
to warn
against community from afar.

Each name constructed with multiple stones.
Each name
broken down to rocks
the size of two grasping hands.
The rocks
handpicked, transported, tinted,
laid to rest in the shape of a name.

Multitudinous,
the name expresses itself only in plurals,
always exaggerations.

Repurposed, repatriated,
stones estranged in new names.

Names > words

Word
is to become
word is woord
which is not a word in
English
Engels
angels
> <

Scant undulation of landscape
which is not mountain
but towers over the town.
If it is not a mountain, it is not a meaning.

It is terrain as introduction,
a vacancy
to clarification.

Verklaring

Vertolking

Klippertjies…

Skip
words over the landscape
as it were
a lake.

Confusing when lake is *meer* in Afrikaans
but *mer* is sea in French but *See* is lake in German
and *meer* is more
and *See* is sight.

Up close
rocks are the reverse of flowers.
Flowers in the semi-desert
shine, tiny pin-pricks of white between grays and browns.
The rocks are blanched, spotted with brown
where the paint peels
through to its original self peering out
as negative space
lichen.

Distanced,
disintegration looks cohesive.
On site, standing between words, letters deform, rocks roll away.
Names camouflage in vegetation.
Proximity instigates uniformity.

Changing a name to the exact same name
requires an insanity of signage,
new documents and maps à la carte.
Identity politics of place.
Luxuriating ululations in the throat.

Racializing script
is like saying the skeleton is sexual to the bone.

                                      Rock hard
                                      Kliphard
                                      Clip art
                                      Klip
                                      Cliff
                                      Of
                                      Or(e)
                       ——————— or no ———————
                                      Knoll
                                      Nil
                                      Niks

Tangible but illegible
my concentration dissolves toward the cacti,
alien growth, thorny /
throaty
limbs
asking to / akin to

Hand
in
hand.

2

STILLFRAME INBOX[1]

In a box of stones, weight hangs limp on a scale.
When you lie on top of me without holding your own muscles
in place, your mass relaxes to an untenable crash.
I'm told her face was beautiful, but her hands invisible
and I imagine her ghostly as in old paintings
where a face materializes from a very dark background
and her body is almost unseen within the technical bonds of cerements.
To me this image explains why while writing
the previous poem months ago I considered alluding
to my friend's street art stone project but ultimately didn't—
weaning myself from beloved topics
is one of my unsuccessful attempts at discarding
what I think I write and then writing exactly the same stuff.
I always think boxes are for safekeeping
little caskets of treasures, traditionally precious stones and diamonds,
bone china or home-blown glass dildos, not rocks
a collection of chunks
that just happen to be present and emotionally available.
This is girl time and we're painting rocks (rock paintings)
brushing camouflage on stones to stand out—
layering the tops, laying them down to dry, colouring their underbellies,
scatterbrained under the bridge by the railway tracks.
Perhaps it's a corrective to my startled state of mind
that faults are found in the dull thuds resounding
as we throw stones below the underpass from a bucket
swinging our arms, one by one, for further reach
or dropping the stones right by our feet.
It's not safe sex, location is everything and this place
is not the wrong side of the tracks but the tracks themselves
where trains no longer make their elated way
and men walk tracing exhalations in the dust with their boots
going home to loved ones as I say shit under my breath
and she's like *my bra* which means brother and not otherwise.

Apparently exposing the buttocks
is more offensive than bare breasts or so I'm told by locals.
I never thought of myself as breasted till
I was told so and since then I've felt threatened and apologetic.
It's a real breakthrough when I realize
the ass is one entity and must not be shaped as two perfectly round balls
straddled by the hips—rectangular continuity,
delicious licentiousness.

The image is called Desperately Disciplined.
It is of a woman reading on her stomach on a couch
a beautiful position
with her head on her hand and fingers flattening the spine of the text,
feet rubbing up against or rubbing each other the wrong way.
Like a couple, this is actually an uncomfortable pose
compromising for appearances:
the neck pinches, the back arches too far,
the head weighs down upon the wrist, red lines form.
The difficulty of paging forward while keeping the book open
is decadent and erudite, but only for a while.
This work, leaping from so-called property defacement
to aspiration as ambition as just pronouncing those breaths
correctly on gallery walls.
It's a painting, an animation, a stop-frame animation,
one brushstroke at a time, it's a canvas projection,
a series of stillframe prints, tagged, papered, pasted across the town.
The conversation goes something along the line of sketches,
the intensity of thinning the thickness sickening patches of graphite,
graffiti is the tongue you're willing to tie (or not)
it's a mode of expression with no signature, modus operandi on mission creep.
Sometimes, posturing, the muscles in my shoulders
assume the characteristics of a cloak
and my dagger is a reminder
we discuss potential shades of verbatim.

Still
stillframe
is another title altogether
for urgency in the moment of immobility
rises to the eyelids an awareness of physical limits
these days I've been framing all my art in white.

She always had better responses to politics than me
and it's too bad that I can't remember these.

The dead artist is on repeat.
Whereas everything between us begins with a reproduction[2]
her work is condemned to develop only as reproduction—
vitality is outdated, novelty not an option, creation numbered,
unnumbing is passing off someone else's vision as one's own.
I have always wanted video art in my home
the work in motion, on repeat, in a loop
the strange logistics of wish fulfillment
including a television screen, mountings, electric bills
and cords inbuilt or trailing down the walls.
Rock art falls hard
naturally too weighty I read natal
that boulder acting itself is having just as hard a time as I have acting myself.
Biologically inclined to anthropomorphize the artwork,
this is sculptural,
the form in the stone, the formed stone, the man in the moon.
Statistically there is the possibility of a one-dimensional statue.
Business as usual reading images with intuition,
when things become systematically more real during morning coffee
an image speaks and I fondle words analphabetic in the palm,
check what lies beneath, perhaps nothing more than the surface.
At least in a claustrophobic space you know your limits[3]
and in the cave of the subconscious
pictograms sit still in their outlines
stasis being one way to see self-confidence.
When the image lies on the proverbial couch and recounts its tribulations
it is the sofa
room
surroundings which remove their clothes
whereas the image remains solid
stolid
this fight, your dislike countered by the fact it is mine.
At least you must be open to the unconventional placement of furniture
tracing face-off with fingertips.
This museum is for touch.

The subtitle in contemporary art
is the subtle rivalry of stillness and activity
involving time, the ability to arrest the viewer, to stand for the entire duration
stop-frame / animation
that beautiful contradiction
in which the continued existence of another in yourself
is the only real definition of the hereafter.

Die videos wat jy vir my stuur wil nie hier speel nie
gee net vir my sulke skewe gesiggies :-/

3

LAS MENINAS[4]

My writing is like
male nudes in the Western tradition of art
soft, even the strongest most beautiful man.
I lie / recline
my writing is erect
in the smallest possible way
taut but not extended suggestive
then discontinued to the potential reach of the image.

Whereas hands can touch / mouths can touch
eyes cannot touch.
Eye contact
is too naked to bear scrutiny, an eye for an eye isn't physical
the uncertainty around catching someone's eye—
you could think you looked at each other with intention
but then looked aside
eyes darting
between the portrait which is the face and the landscape which is life
organs so open they have to close from time to time
with a fleeting shudder / shut
glistening
vulnerable undress.

Las Meninas
appears in my reading coincidentally,
repeatedly, a travel scenario[5],
the traveller a woman whose lover says she resembles the Velázquez lass
then seeing the recreation by Pablo Picasso.
A poet[6] writes essays about Eros
describes the blind spot
into which the girls are staring / staring down the gaze.
The curation of my reading list morphs into an actual gallery
of images, am
I conscious of the fame
before other authors point me in visual / visionary directions?
Las Meninas is a whole lot of little girls.
The central girl is a conduit,
natural light falls like a blessing directly on her temples
or emanates naturally from her, angelic
she does not stand she hovers.
Compare Rembrandt's De Nachtwacht
that little girl luminescent
locks like wings
halo a vision in the gloom.
The unsightly girl, her face recreated as a moon in the other picture,
a negative space in the gloaming.
Could there be an understudy for the infanta?
Stripping beneath the dress that takes up so much space
layers and layers of maidenhood negligee.
Make sure she structurally blows.

In the monochromatic room
crowded with antiques, placed furnishings, pieces of value
I hope that somewhere I am still burdened with a fragment of girlhood.
Fragrances with which he photographs,
postures are just ways of laying out the body
the wake in an objective observance
fear of being caught out
in flagrante delicto
sofa bed occasional
sheets and needing / kneeling to pray.
He always offers one image
to the sitter
thanks for posing
proposing nothing is the right way to let her down easy.

Every night I imagine his body either in front or behind mine.
I sleep on my side.
When he is behind me, his arm reaches over my waist
and I should feel protected
but I feel safer when pressing my defenseless front against his back
breathing the air
from the warm division between us.

Emptiness is an edge / on edge / an edge
these little feminist anatomies.
I disallow my body from others
skin is way too porous a vessel for what it contains.
On the subject of nakedness most suppose
an aesthetic agreement:
to pose is to yield your outline to a definition of beauty
to hope that something good will come of it
the disappointment of body
will be elevated, lasting, a lofty homage to self.
No one I know longs to look worse.
Taking off my clothes is a form of in flight hygiene
cleanliness cakes to the skin, nudity shamed for its divinity
being imagined as being
larger than life
disproportionate glorious
gorgeous anonymous
when nobody knows you anymore
and everything locks stoically to the perspective
of an
unassisted eye / naked eye.
The maids of honour are those pictured in the nude.

Picasso undresses the Velázquez girls.
This is not perverted.
He takes things away from them—wealth
the contrived innocence of their faces / the healthy glow in the cheeks
he takes away the ceiling, the quiet space, the dictated focus
fills the space with calculated disarray
robes and the painter
all curves like a male version of woman
smaller curves
moustache
ceremonial insignia
stimulus muse
light.
In interpretation he is no longer a self-portrait
deus ex machina coat check
here and there Velázquez towers like a champ.

I intended this poem to be way more brute force it's fine art let
the décolletage breathe deeper than the neckline.

4

EKKE

I eke
out a meaning for my self.

Ek
Ek
Ek
Ek
Ek
Ek
Stottering
Stutter ringing
sharp / peals of smiles at the attempt / contempt
the temptation to become myself is great.

We're on such intimate terms, when he writes me, he says hi K,
I did not give him leave to abbreviate
me
he takes the initiative
to do in the rest of my spelling.

My name is embedded in my pronoun.

K Afr
C Anglophone / mobile phone / peripatetic cp. very pathetic
One of the first things I learn is that Afrikaans rarely uses Cs
sees
sien
seen everything.

A mirror image is never static.
No still photograph reverses itself, modulates
or rearranges its face, unless it is another picture altogether.
The possibility exists that K reflects C
in a way that has bent or curved one letter
into a resemblance of another.

One of the first things I learn is that English rarely uses K,
except in a CK combination
lock.
Rotate the numbers till chimera and metal gives off on fingertips
tieties in die wind
words kiss but never uncover any form of hidden meaning
unless that meaning is the meaning in that moment
momentum
memento mori.

It is the K in my name that saves me.
K in me *ek*
C is meek.

There are certain associations I harbour against Clara
too British
too Victorian
sweet virtuous desirous / heroine solely in a nuclear family way
complicit in characterization
eyes cast down
passive except for good deeds, dead perhaps.
Conceded there is clarity in Clara but claustrophobic
her beauty is in the innocence of hair lying like unravelling lace on her chest.
Her chastity is duty
her aesthetic ethics
knowledge is restricted to goodness.
The perfect equilibrium, when she
lowers her eyes it is modesty, when I
fail in eye
contact
it's a skittishness, a fault
an unsocialized character / default blank slate.
Connect the dots of our eyes when we chat.

I shame my sister name because I
sense the same gentleness cum submission in me.
If you close the wide open legs of the K, she becomes a cross / *kruis*
reclining
a position of art
submission but with intention
what after all is the difference between gentleness and gentility
a certain crossness in the chirography.

Coincidentally, at the exact moment I consider writing my name
I read about another kind of Clara,
modernized, which means still not quite contemporary.
An artist,
she demands respect in a way that implies erudition but with pride,
self-conscious negation, no-nonsense drapery dresses.
Steeds nie
klinkklaar nie.
Die klankbaan konglomereer om die ore
'n skrikbeeld van oorbelle
mond oorblyfsels teen die skedel
ancestry perverted as
vertes

Ekke is 'n nadruksvorm van ek.

'n Dialek

I am an emphasis of myself.

I speak languages.
Lyftaal
Skryftaal
Statuary marble
constructing my mouth and biting words out in frieze.

In my handwriting "more" often looks like "move."
Handskrif
Tydskrif
Move somehow in time.
I want to spell hand- with more pretension like a playwright.

My language
is a secret / secretion
curled up in a recess
uncurling its animal muscles when the break is done
and auditorium bells chime *dier dierbaar baarmoeder*
mother tongue licks, licks cryptically
from the crypt inside me.
Afrikaans is an affection
hidden / *geheim*
I know for a fact that Heim is home in another language
the finger that sticks its tongue right in there
to break my hymen.

Deciduous female figures
cast off selves
left and right
lies grow out of shoulder blades
and lodge / a nervous condition called the angelic

ekke
is an extension
attached to the back or to dial a direct call

ek ke
back-to-back
ek ek
k lyk soos vlerke.
Forget what I say most of the time
thing is, he listens, he thinks.
When lovers lie back-to-back there is dust on things they'll never clean
their bodies inflecting wings.
Ekke
is not a mirror reflection
but it is a reflection.

Spelling
Spieël
Speel
Spel

The mirror is not a safe space.
When I look in the mirror I see / C
reflections of language.
It is prejudiced against me
I do not belong in any one mirror, my tongue licks away the definition
of language in the mist on the glass
the glass responds differently when I ask in different lingos
there is no lingua franca of the mind
my kind
jou taal is ontwortel
gegordel
'n gegorrel
genade tog
I got to go.

5 CONVEYOR BELT

die

beeste.

Die beste.
The best beasts pass slowly on a linear movable road.
Sometimes it spontaneously detours
into a Lynch-like[7] highway,
dirt track,
skywalk,
or a black line leading tarred to the abattoir.
Pull yourself together till a narrow thread
becomes a chronological timeline to hang yourself
not for naught
the morbidity built into the definite article,
die like slaughter is a means to an end.
Die
Daai
That blessed with so many meanings
███
for sure meat is not supposed to bruise.
I wish that words would bear the definitions I give them
baptism right on the hairless front
████████████
█████████████████████
████████
████████████

blessure
if *bles* could be connected to *blessure*
and wound could be undone by the backward rotation of
████████████

the word I'm looking for is the best possible word—
alias, some bestiality.

Breasts
with their eternal asymmetrical pairings
one a little larger, little lower, little more slide to the side.
Ask me which denomination I prefer for my junk
ranging from formal to crude
and I say
borste
bored stiff.
Bors borrel vol
soos 'n fool *pof bors*
plofbaar is die bees sonder horings
horny necessity accompaniment to revelatory
horn blowing. Revelling
in the number of the beast
is something I've never cared about but some obsess over,
the correct number of breasts
should be two
although one does hear of unusual cases
three or four even with pictures
poniekoerante
gossip columns.

Colostrum
is the first milk produced by a woman after her calf is born.
My calves rigid from walking far I have seen everything
travelling I am never known to take the conveyor belt feels too much a continuation
of the illusion we're not perpetually in motion.
Beestings is a synonym richer in antibodies.
During pregnancy she refers to herself as ▮cow
suppose multiple stomachs would allow to
birth and rebirth the baby
▮dresses so large she doubles her size expands beyond belief
▮▮▮▮▮▮▮▮▮ pumping out mammary glands
to freeze substance and later fertilize her infant through the throat.

A road is an entrance
at any cross section of its length
a chain of events,
guiding light,
bit
into the mouthpiece.
Sometimes I need to girdle what I write. Bridle / bridal
the wedding gown a cultural expanse
written in milk, invisible ink, then singed to make words visible.
The groom brushes down the horse / neglects to brush down the cow.

~~I am not in wedlock with a country~~
~~when asked the difference between the lands I inhabit~~ inhibit
~~as if inquiring the time~~
~~only ever answer the landscape is so attractive~~
~~*doodgetrek*~~
~~skyline always crossed out *toegetrek*~~
~~like curtains natural beauty a way to sidestep doorstop~~
~~everything else of consequence I should invoke the minotaur~~
~~*Nguni klei koei* maiden name~~
~~cows cover up their shame by default~~
~~strolling in their natural habitat~~
~~*koeie*~~ quiver ~~*klitsgras knapsekêrels*~~
~~knapsack for steak filet sirloin~~
~~roast ribs mince~~
~~oxtail tongue~~-tied
cows cowed by bullying bulls
~~beefed up bodybuilt guilt~~
~~to hold up heaven celestial impasse~~
~~I walk beneath it in the flesh~~
~~*vlees vleis vleiend*~~ veiled
~~flattery is a type of language greenery versant drinking it~~
~~in verbal flânerie~~

I walk across different languages as if they are flatlands
veld / felt like
origins are lost en route
destination a deletion that leaves no trace.
Editing out is less a line than an exemption.
Emptiness could be anywhere, you wouldn't even know it
oopte / leegte / leemte / te is too much.
If you manhandle language, like other things, it cowers.

[I want to conjugate the cow.

I
Io
Isis]

Domesticated animals most often live in a form
an enclosure like a field or a pen
pen different identities
down on the ground
cattle catalogue
bul, os, koei, kalf
in Afrikaans
heifer renders as *vers*
vers also being the strophe of a poem.
It is one of the most beautiful literary definitions that a poem is an untouched cow.

[Io is the one
transformed into a cow for being loved by a god.
I always imagine her more delicate
calves tapering out to hooves
those long gloves
with the suggestion of skin where the leather won't grow.
Virginity behooves her.]

[
The udder
is the other woman.
Begin by censoring the offensive bits,
blocking them out in every image
black rectangle which is the teats
teetering on the edge of is and is
no one can expect to be the exact same way twice.
The nipples dot the I
squirting long white lines.
Nourishment is a *genadelose dood* ode to absolutely everything else.
One of the most terrible things is to bury a goddess in the cool box.
]

6

HUNTER-GATHERER CRIMINALS

"a given"

the prerogative of what we think we have a right to

The man who is not a hunter
stands on his graying front lawn and flexes
his rifle. It's an elephantine instrument
meant for larger than life faces
that are really portraits on loan for a lifetime.
His intention is to impress, his pose verbose, his laughter
accessory to some crime on the mind.
The man at my side has disfigured my confidence,
followed me over continents, avowed words in my mouth
that left me in the incomplete semicircle of his arms.
Everyone seems to think it's okay if you
eat what you hunt or to hunt / pursue who you want,
but the expiration date on aggression is long gone.
The more she asks if I'm offended the more she offends me.
Clearly there are alternate ways to attack
that do not draw blood, draw a weapon, or draw near—
even writing no longer carves words into paper,
rather touches keys with fingertips.
The repertory cinema of violence casually credits everyone
at the ending.

Hunt stands adjacent to hurt
to be protected is to let that person be exposed.
Show-off of masculinity and suddenly
there's a collection of men, a natural history museum right there and then.

My hometown houses a museum of language.
Such beautiful architecture,
solid, symmetrical flanks, ornamental limbs
and an ancient orange grove (soon uprooted) with perfect
bright yellow circles adorning the branches.
I pluck at juice around the mouth.
We wander up to the clock tower and stay there
playing childhood games that all involve being unseen
in a world together but private.
The orbs of dead authors egg us on—
histoire de l'œil[8] is attention deficit disorder in hindsight
and my hands are dismayed, key in lock, as we secretly
explore the exhibitions unattended. NALN
stands for *Nasionale Afrikaanse Letterkundige Navorsingsentrum*
which does not mean museum but does mean research centre which does not
seem dead which is why it does not only mean language but literature.

To reminisce is a ritual.
But to renew
a book at the library or the cells of the skin
or for a nation to officiate one language to eleven
is the hardest doubling act you'll see
from   1   to   11 —
it's the death sentence / pagination / museum / mausoleum
in this country.

My hometown
is an indecent display case.
A black box that conceals its apparatus, runs on invisible laws,
lawns input registered history
products put on pedestals and monuments, adornments, defilements,
dedications, cake-stands and men as busts.
The museum is filled with black boxes.
Glass is passé.

Some kinds of glass partitions warp the view through.
Some kinds of eyes warp their own points of view.

To invest in transparency
to no longer frequent those cafés, to commit to my hood,
to heed the intended future
memory hovers like heaven helps no one.
In my hometown a museum hangs on a hook on the wall.
Inhuman humanism canvassing
recollections to become an immaculate collection.
A gathering is most often a collection of persons
sometimes aesthetic but rarely functional.
The beauty and formality of the display case incubator
in which relations are not born but eternalized
in which gestures castrate
in which humanity mutates
in which a new influx of tendencies
tender in the complete frigidity of do not touch / do not feel.
It was the first time I saw him cry.

Tears have their own agenda
they mark the walls of the cheeks,
schedule a meeting with dissatisfaction, rip through rest in peace.
The gesture of wiping tears from beneath the eyes is universal—
pictures blur my face, unfocused facets of cut glass,
the resignation
of looking through life rather than at images still stuck in a book.
In literature adults shake the fetus as a light form of corporal punishment.
In grief the shake autogenerates as a masochistic ritual
that pretends to be empathetic, then repeats.
Emotion is lonely.
Localized in the body
grief is deadly, but at least an honestly physical experience
in which the body feels deflated reaching out—
departmentalized, sculptural and fluid.

When he says she's territorial I don't quite know what he means,
but can guess.
The body does not want to be a spectacle
and yet everything falls apart through the eyes.

In my notes hunter-gatherer is abbreviated to h.g.
I fill in the blanks so it looks like hunger
these notes written on receipts, the white unused backsides of paper,
sales tickets prompting what I put into my mouth.
What comes out of my mouth grows from the seeds planted in my guts,
tendrils coursing, blossoms frothing and fruit thudding
to the floor from my face.
It's a whole new obsession this cultivation by means of orifice
feeding the population each from their own
pulling vegetation from between the teeth
then replacing it to ruminate.
The stomach a somatic terrarium
that functions as a protective glass vial
a safe space from which to scale the throat,
direct these plants that flourish as they drop anchor
eager to please, flowing to the ground.
They grow reptilian / greenery skin
bile just word of mouth.
Considering now the lush but enclosed change of landscape
I'm definitely thinking of Rappaccini's Daughter[9].

The weather conditions are currently calm / wet, so stay indoors,
but not too cold or too humid,
a consistency of temperature not changing much night to day.
Time mellows its following
and the soft rain just soaks in to nourish.

This rainbow nation[10]
favouring the monochrome colour scheme
of black, white, and at most, brown.

Race is a script quite literally
last night I told genre it's looking pretty normal and it was pleased.

7

CEILING ROSES

For Serena Thomson

/

The implication if I use the noun rose
in lieu of the verb.
Never misspelling a thing, arranging arousal like flowers.

/

She tells me he told her that flowers
should only be arranged in uneven numbers.
On a prearranged day of the week he offers up
three or five or seven flowers
to the vase.
Roses are never very far from   the other
's access to lace.

/

Things to place in vases—

Flour ashes
Dissensions
Negative space
Not for naught
The inner narrative of an urn
Contemporaneously all poetry
Headers on dashes
Shapeless mess of emotion
Verb and verb constructions (I sit and write)
Filigree of ceiling rose arrangements
Electric stems lit descending before another god gets lost
god se beentjie being

Are these a gift or for you?
For me.

/

Thank god we fact-checked the name
for botanic and botanical gardens
have ambivalent meanings.
When the poet steps on stage and suggests
that immigrant and emigrant might be the same,
I want to rough up exegesis before everyone
but decency intervenes and the distance between thrusts
lingers.

/

Long-stemmed high-rises
thorns thread
shed
slit
of shears and other data I don't know's necessary.

/

City of roses[11]
placeholder for growing up
fold up
hometown
this is no term of endearment
but an actual epithet
gaan julle blommetjies, blommetjies maak
in desert conversational
flowers hold moisture firmly between thumb and index.

/

The social ceiling
secular rosary, road rage
is the most unattractive thing.
The glass ceiling
transparent minorities
mounting/s
the uppermost fixture/s of the room
pearl thongs along
lay myths down man.

8

SOMEONE OTHER THAN ELSE

This was the title I proposed
when somebody drew my portrait from a hat—
it seemed so easy and realistic,
but had really been crafted with meticulous affection.
The colours are black, red and brown
with a hint of olive green in the folds of my elbow
and a transparency to the open spaces
suggesting I'm of the most delicate porcelain,
prematurely grown into a person.
This is also an almost identical arrangement
of colours to Antonio Saura's Cocktail Party.
Assuming that his title
would originally have been in Spanish,
it's strange how I can't find the name—
not knowing if Cóctel is correct
I have to translate backwards to the authentic
rather than forwards to the projected
potential of an internet generated bit of language.
Alternatively, the name was in English all along,
a sensationalized expat party
populated with languages, revelling in confusion
of cohesion and inclination,
blurring the crisp edges of meaning.
Being a name means you're someone.

The slant of the A
is the crux of my name, I find myself
explaining (surrounded, socially enshrouded)
again. The upwardly mobile, North American
alpha A—mounting in cutthroat tenor—
contrasts with the soft diminuendo of vowel,
the lowering of tone
of how to actually say—

/ ' kl ær ɑ /
/ ' kl ɑːr ɑ /

Words are sounds that sometimes pretend to have meaning.

Skemerkelkie
is the equivalent of a mixed drink.
The first half meaning dusk,
to sip at the onset of sunset.
Yet there is literally no translation
sufficiently beautiful to convey *kelk*
almost the same pronunciation as the first syllable
of *quelque chose*, but lacking something—
the floral instinct, the tubular grace of a lily,
the insinuation of petals opening,
fingers cupping in nocturnal gestures.
An antique evening vase of alcohol
carries only a fraction of the pensiveness missing
from the glamour and shrill laughter
of a cocktail party /
cocktail panty like a little garnish to the night.

This is an interdisciplinary
soirée.
I envision small talk in cursive,
beautiful squiggles,
full circle palm beaches,
men full-frontal
with their subtropical strap-ons.
Knockout moments of dressing-up or down
the in-between space diminishing drastically
as feet tread the floor
and dreadful sentiments seem sexy inebriated.
Don't go, please don't go
have another drink.
There's the wrap-around of arms,
the intimacy of staring
slant into the eyes of a stranger.
What if we were friends,
if this acceptance were a thing?
Please don't go
a supplication to consort.
Being socialized is knowing
when parties devolve to monosyllabic
communication moments of wow.
Everything we do is shared in version repartee.

You take me by the shoulders saying
thank you,
thank you for being there for me.
Thank you for being there for me / when I need to write
about you.

As night slips into sunlight
and images reveal their artists, home
assumes a wondrous sense of otherness.
I say important things with my lips
pressed up against the rim of a vase,
whisperingly inarticulate. Cardiac
is an unpleasant way of thinking of the heart,
textbook bedside manner, considering love
thumping and shuddering
ethically
to always put life first.
As I lie here now, felt up
in complete tenderness, it occurs to me
that my body drops like a wave,
breasts trickling off my chest, thighs fighting
then collapsing, spreading, expanding
and thinning out, limpid and clear,
before retracting, climbing into themselves,
refining their pores
a pool of water collecting itself solemnly
to return to solidity.
The difference between inundate and undulate
is so slim, yet I master it
within the time bracket it takes to pour this glass
of water and drink it.

TRANSLATIONS

from Afrikaans to English, unless otherwise specified

1. FIRST OF ALL WE NO LONGER WRITE IN BLACK

word is woord	becoming is word
Engels	English
Verklaring	definition
Vertolking	interpretation
Klippertjies	small stones / gravel
meer	lake / more
mer (French)	sea
See (German)	lake
Kliphard	rock-hard
Klip	stone
Of	or
Niks	nothing
hand	hand

2. STILLFRAME INBOX

my bra	my brother (colloquial)

Die videos wat jy vir my stuur wil nie hier speel nie
gee net vir my sulke skewe gesiggies :-/

The videos you send me won't play here
just give me these skew little faces :-/

4. EKKE

Ekke	a dialectic, emphatic form of *ek*, similar to French, "*moi, je...*"
Ek	I
Stottering	stuttering
sien	sees
tieties in die wind	tits in the wind
kruis	cross

Steeds nie
klinkklaar nie.
Die klankbaan konglomereer om die ore
'n skrikbeeld van oorbelle
mond oorblyfsels teen die skedel
ancestry perverted as
vertes

Still no
absolute clarity.
The soundtrack conglomerates about the ears
a dread image of earrings
mouth remnants against the skull
ancestry perverted as
vistas

Ekke *is 'n nadruksvorm van ek.*
'n Dialek

Ekke is an emphasis of I.
A dialect

Lyftaal	body language
Skryftaal	written language

Handskrif   handwriting
Tydskrif   magazine (but also literally time-writing)
dier dierbaar baarmoeder animal, cute / beloved, womb
geheim   secret
Heim (German)   home

k lyk soos vlerke   k resembles wings

Spieël   mirror
Speel   play
Spel   spell / game

my kind
jou taal is ontwortel
gegordel
'n gegorrel
genade tog
I got to go.

my child
your language is uprooted
girdled
a gurgling
for goodness sake
I got to go.

5. CONVEYOR BELT

die   the
beeste   cattle

Die beste   the best
Daai   those (colloquial form of *daardie*)
blessure (French)   wound
bles   bald

borste   breasts

Bors borrel vol
soos 'n fool *pof bors*
plofbaar is die bees sonder horings

Chest bubble-full
like a puffed up fool
explosive is the beast without horns

poniekoerante	gossip columns / tabloids (literally pony newspapers)
~~*doodgetrek*~~	deleted
~~*toegetrek*~~	shut
~~*Nguni klei koei*~~	Nguni clay cow
~~*koeie*~~	cows
~~*klitsgras*~~	burdock
~~*knapsekêrels*~~	blackjacks
~~*vlees vleis vleiend* veiled~~	flesh, meat, flattering, veiled
veld	veld
oopte / leegte / leemte / te	open space / emptiness / lack / too
bul, os, koei, kalf	bull, ox, cow, calf
vers	heifer / verse or poem
genadelose dood	merciless death

6. HUNTER-GATHERER CRIMINALS

Nasionale Afrikaanse Letterkundige Navorsingsentrum
National Afrikaans Literary Museum and Research Centre

7. CEILING ROSES

god se beentjie	god's bone (diminutive) / god's leg (diminutive)

gaan julle blommetjies, blommetjies maak
blossoms, will you flower? (baby talk)

8. SOMEONE OTHER THAN ELSE

Cóctel (Spanish)   cocktail party
Skemerkelkie   cocktail (literally dusk-glass)
quelque chose (French)   something

NOTES

1. "Stillframe Inbox" is based on an artwork by my friend Dorothea (Dot) Vermeulen, tragically deceased in 2015, called Desperately Disciplined.

2. Jacques Derrida, *The Postcard: From Socrates to Freud and Beyond.*

3. Louise Bourgeois, *Strukturen des Daseins: Die Zellen.*

4. "Las Meninas" is based on Diego Velázquez's painting and Pablo Picasso's version of it.

5. Lynne Tillman, *Motion Sickness.*

6. Anne Carson, *Eros The Bittersweet.*

7. David Lynch.

8. Georges Bataille.

9. Nathaniel Hawthorne.

10. "Rainbow nation" is a term coined by Desmond Tutu to describe multiculturalism in post-Apartheid South Africa.

11. Byname of Bloemfontein, South Africa, where I grew up.

ACKNOWLEDGEMENTS

Thank you to landscapes, spaces, and paintings, without which writing would be harder. Thank you to Jim Johnstone and Palimpsest Press for transforming a manuscript into a book; aan Hendrik du Plessis en die woord "deursigtigheid"; aan Jean Dreyer wie nog altyd gesê het ek sal 'n boek hê teen 30; to Dean Garlick for day-to-day gentleness; to friends and poets for community.

"Las Meninas" received third place for the *words(on)pages* 2016 Blodwyn Memorial Prize, and was subsequently included in Issue 15 of *(parenthetical)*, September 2016.

"Ekke" was previously published in *Asymptote*'s July 2016 Multilingual Issue.

"Ceiling Roses" appeared in Issue 33 of *The Puritan*, Spring 2016.

PHOTO: DEAN GARLICK

Klara du Plessis is a poet and critic. Residing in Montreal, but growing up in Bloemfontein, South Africa, Afrikaans is her first language and its coexistence with English while writing embodies a personal form of linguistic honesty. Klara's chapbook *Wax Lyrical*—shortlisted for the bpNichol Chapbook Award—was released by Anstruther Press in 2015. Poems, essays, and reviews have appeared in print and online. She curates the monthly, Montreal-based Resonance Reading Series and is the editor for *carte blanche*.